I0571203

Dog:
The Anatomy of Need

By *Natalya Ziska*
2025

Cover: Still Life with Flowers, Grapes, and Small Game Birds - Frans Snyder
(1615)

<u>you are here</u>

i. *Digging*

1-Crown Roast

Curl Up
Nose Blind I
The Wolf and The Rabbit
About Creation
Concrete

2-The Heart

Sacral Desire
Red String I
Roots
Time
To my Marbled Lover
Hunt
A Gift from Desire

3-(and Other Offal)

Stare
The Wolf and the Hare
Word Scraps
Red String II
Loathe
Hunger in Threes

4-Butterfly Loin

The Floor
Nose Blind II
A Poet
Red String III
Lost Dog

i. Digging

A wet slobbery nose pushes back dewed dirt to take a sharp
inhale of something sweet, somewhat savory, that sits right
beyond grasp. Swift scoops make their way from the ground,
tenderized meat lingers at the nostril, begging to know teeth.
The rocks begin to hurt as they are ripped from the Earth. But a
hungry hand never stops.

The dust that coats the lungs smells of familiarity; something I
am desperate to grab, desperate to understand, so close and yet
unattainable.
I need it, I need you to understand it; the feel, the smell, the
taste–the delicate, simple, deep tastes.
This selfish hope of reaction urges on the ideas of peeling fowl
skins–those soaked limp, in brown butter and rosemary, buried
right beneath the tongue. The notion of satisfaction and delight
in the distance.
The wish I wish for you: to dance ravenously with violins as you
eat this animal with your bare hands, every fine oil, fat, and
sugar rubbed together between the creases that make up you.
You beautiful thing.
I want you to recognize the words made up of lemon zest and
herbs. Feel them sting your throat; find them in the ground.
Invisible flavors that make you starve–that make you understand
this feeling.

I don't understand the cycle of which I need, want, or desire.
But the perpetual drum drives me to dig up these holes in the
yard; carry these ridged and bloodied hands, with a mouth
edging on rabid.

What a beast I would be if I weren't scared to cross the trees or bite the lamb.

Crown Roast

to all that is a cage

Curl Up

When my face was softer, when my hands were unwashed,
when I was unable to see over that granite countertop:
I would curl up in the center of my bed like an animal.
Craving something bigger than I was,
an illusion of carnal blood through the eyes of a child,
laying still, atop the clean sheets of concealed dirt.

You'll find something to do with your hands,
scratch the surface with something beautiful, again.
Curl up, sleep there, next to the clock you pulled apart,
next to the pages of dreams scribbled down,
and the ink you'll leave stained on your leg another week.
Let these scattered insides
and secret synchronicities lull you to sleep, again.

Young, I'd already fear the prosaic world outside my room,
as my itchy skin protested daily.
So to lay as an animal, restful in the earth,
I could falsely conceal the concrete sun.

Nose Blind I

The warm plot of land where the sun lays hot and shining,
where you can see every strand of grass, down to the root,
treating you with coherent consistency.
Each blade–a thing, a thought, an object.

This patch, well loved, well known,
where your muscle memory controls the day.
The left turn to work, the words, the writings:
subject, add, add, send.
Face, hand, word, concrete.
Another piece of grass.

Borrowed hands twist and pull each blade,
rolling out the green chloroplastic liquids each day,
while your eyes drift and linger on the overgrown greenery
unrelenting, planes of grass, trees, herbs and
the unknowing of things.

Check on your hands, they're there,
they're yours, you can do anything.

The Wolf and The Rabbit

Your gaze felt like a mirror, telling me we are the same,
while your footprints were oddly hard to follow.
I stopped asking, after you cried,
if my feet were just smaller.

If our hearts are the same,
and our eyes are the same,
then we are the same.

Still, each step, each fumble,
you assured it'd be easier if you carry me,
so I let you.
You said *it's so cold, here,*
get into my mouth,
and I trusted you.
Because I thought we had the same
heart, the same eyes,
I thought your advice was derived from care.
And I looked past your differing teeth.

But now I fear your eyes,
the way they flinch at my words.
If I say the wrong thing
your jaw clenches down further.
And I only just noticed.

About Creation

The table before me has grown bland.
Lazily made of splintering wood
and desaturated by the tired air.
My skin, the walls–looking of plaster;
decaying hands made of silver.

But I'm stuck on the plate.

A glimmering porcelain, lined in gold,
brush strokes of green and red depicting succulent flowers,
and atop it,
a pristine white cake, sliced clean,
specked with juicy red strawberries, and
fluffed cream placed in clean delicate swirls.

It sits, still as dead,
as I do, staring.

Concrete

A concrete slab has fallen on my hand.
Pinned me to the ground, twenty-seven bones lingering.
This pristine off-white block, coarse and heavy,
tastes of bleak dust compared to the grass stuck in my teeth.
My arm stings at the thought of my immobile hand,
the fragments entertaining the idea of being sown,
a sensation hidden from me.

To now struggle like a mouse in a trap:
caged to the stomach of another,
where kindled metal surrounds all but the skin,
salty and glistening in front of you.
Don't mind the screams. Dig so you'll live.
Twist and push, pull and tear,
until flesh becomes menial at last.

Would separation by eager teeth be easier
in the height of epinephrine,
or the lunacy of the wilted hours?

Will you track down each vein that must part from the hand,
Every word created by it,
tell them they don't belong anymore,
that they'll find newness.
Let them mourn a moment longer.

Don't think about how it happened, think about
how you'll leave. Think about the slab,
the gray that has taken your sanctity.
Twenty-seven bones, and the flesh that helps them,

gone.

Find dirt again.

The Heart

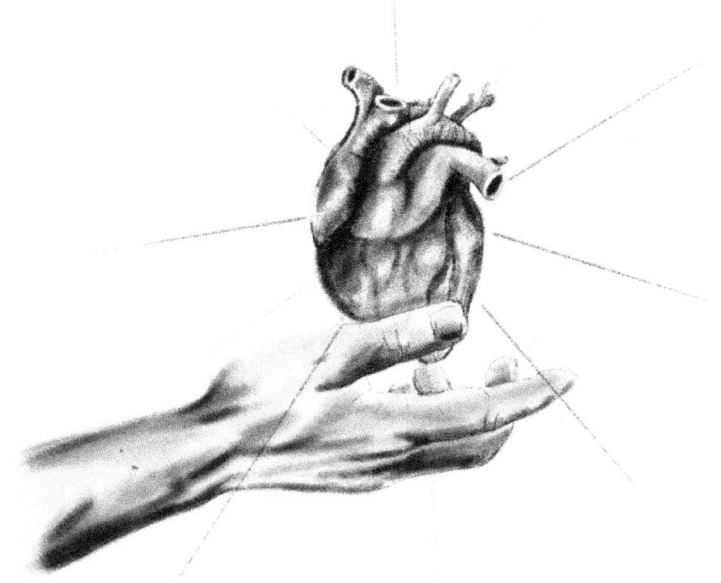

*my favorite words are the
ones made of you*

Sacral Desire

When I showed the priest of how I worship you
I was called unholy.

I was told that my white collared shirts musn't be washed
in the satin of your blood,
that the charcoal lines on temple walls
should depict more than the arch of an indiscernible body part.

After a sermon on your fingertips was carried out past sunset,
he described the way I laid you on the stage,
in a fine night blue sheet, as sacrificial.
Knives ready, for a lamb at the slaughter.

Little does he know, later,
I will be found, my chest bare,
with bones protruding through the skin
remolded by the sacral thoughts of my thumb on your cheek,
looking of cathedrals, sharp edges so intricately laced.

The priest will close his eyes
muttering about the lewdness in nudity,
describing the sour rotting flesh as
a vile display of luciferianism.

How unbearable it is to think
I could worship you,
love you,
adore you,
any less.

Red String I

On my back, laying, staring
at the deep red string hanging over my heart.
From oblivion, its feathered end glows and reaches,
my veins grasping back, like roots.
I feel them talk nightly of how to connect to one another,
how to get inside.

My eyes have begun to water, my stare is endless,
this string is a foot away and moves an inch a year,
but its impact is definite–predetermined.

My fingers graze against my scalp before
a twirling and a yank
pulling out one rich brown thread
and gently weaving it into the string.

All night, my hands weave, my eyes tire,
and soon, the red becomes brown
and the brown becomes skin,
and I become the end of the string.

Roots
(heart/skin/fabric/fabric/skin/heart)

Sometimes I have to hold you as if you just fell from the sky;
as if I knew the sun would explode tomorrow;
as if my body needed yours to survive.
And when I do,

My arms become branches, reaching for you;
                              the sun.
My fingers become roots, intertwining with you;
                              the soil.
And my heart, a bird, trying to find you;
                              the song.

Time

Kiss me hard,
burn the food,
fall to the floor,
relinquish time.
The space between,
you and I and I and you,
Push and pull and dip and drag,
Stretch until we reach the stars.
If I close my eyes and take a deep breath,
I can taste your exhale.

That that's followed by the subtle upward tilt
on the corners of your lips.

To My Marbled Lover

The smell of iron and dust stains as
the heat of light pours in endlessly
caressing your skin, that carved delicately of marble,
as you lay in the center of this overgrown room.

My consciousness traces the burning glow;
up your waist, down your arm, through your fingers.
You look of villainy, riddled with perfections
entertaining the line of divinity.

Howbeit, that the finest oils and acids
lay beneath your surface, generously aged
and mangled in flesh, darling, I'm curious
if I could drive my fingers into your chest.

The fabric I compose keeps
me within your reach. When I eventually nourish the soil
with my heart, may the vines grow
toward you, and teach me of your ivory
once more.

Hunt

Sat, afar, gazing upon the eyes that now tempt you.
The idea of pressure caressing your neck from the teeth, the
lips.
The act of one swift move
relinquishes your muscles, exposes your bones–
the rawness of you showing before your teeth can catch on.

Your lengthy, amber haired, counterpart hidden in the trees,
hidden in the mist of dawn,
will show themselves for a gracious bow.
One of transcendence,
telling tales of similar affinities,
and notes of aging that binds you.

A quick sprint, a racing heart,
an aimless step on twigs, snapping,
cracking, tripping, falling.

Your breath can be seen.
You smell the musk of another,
close. Close enough
to feel the heat of tongue along your neck,
the softness of a bite, one scared to be taken.
You can run your fingers through his hair,
pull him closer,
Let the blood drain into the dirt,
feel the pull of each tendon, one by one.
Meet those blue eyes again.

A Gift from Desire

I've been forced awake, again,
in the salient stillness of the night,
with a burning light penetrating my chest,
lifting me graciously from the earthiness of my bed.
An iridescent depiction of warmth,
surrendering the whispers of my heart
into this picturesque painting.

Such a wrath of my dearest desires displayed.
Those I keep delicately wrapped in this boney cage,
where they now rupture.
A library of you, bare and sweating,
sweet visuals kept by pure admiration,
fueling a tireless god's forced ignition.

While the slides of you overtake my iris,
I'll stay, lingering in the still air,
Watching each moment my fingers have met your skin,
letting the taste burn from my chest.
I'll let my body run raw, sweat and tears,
just to remember again.

Despite the pain,
I hope this god continues
its ruthless descent in showing me
all of you.

(And Other Offal)

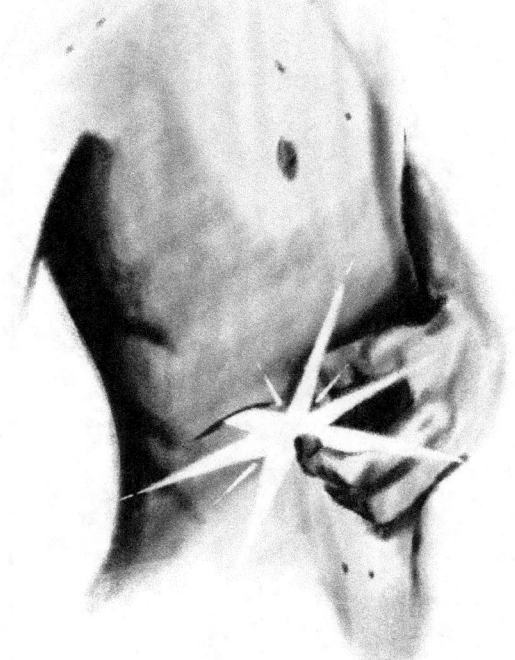

please remove the guts carefully

Stare

I thought you tasted of honey.
You use to give me jars, then spoons,
then a force feed every few months.

I thought you tasted of honey,
until your grin strayed obliquely,
and your eyes used the spoons as knives
to dig out the preconditioned procedures
set, grown, built to maintain your authority.
The structure, employed by honey,
to keep wheels turning for you,
to pressure thoughts into corners,
for you.

It's no wonder, when I tasted real honey,
organically sweet and kind honey,
your machines stopped working.
your wheels stopped spinning.
And I realized, your abstract sugars
have specks of arsenic
and drops of hollowed futures.

You never tasted of honey,
you just figured out how to replicate it.

The Wolf and The Hare

I've felt your bite;
the ways you stopped having to close in
any further to keep me in your jaw.
I, perhaps only a rabbit, would stop asking,
writhing, expressing the discomforts,
as I knew you would only fear the loss of me.

Bite down a little harder, hold me in a little firmer.
So I laid, gut in jaw, as you smiled and waved,
showing me off, having me reach for things.
Never wondering why I stopped disagreeing with you.

I found myself being grateful.
Grateful when you hadn't sharpened your teeth,
grateful when you forgot I was there.
Grateful I could slip out for a moment.

My legs barely knew the ground anymore,
they knew dangling, dangling, limpness,
and I came to know you as your teeth, as your jaw
with ability.

Word Scraps

Sweet dictations.
Plump resources serve up
the rump of a memory.
Caught sinking, slunk down,
behind such tired eyes,
drag devilish rags of flesh to the sea.
Taut rope tied about the waist
to hoist you down, hull you up
and spill the words of voided thoughts,
cleansed with salt and charred bones.
Slip from the skin, become slick and red,
tell yourself you can start again.

Red String II

A gracious tug, and a lifted chest.
There are teeth breaking through the skin of my arm,
digging into the bone to keep a tight hold,
and my darling red string, engrained deep within,
tries to pull me back. Tries to save me.

My heels dig deep lines in the mud
as my mind mutates the ideas
of my mangled hand into some holy sacrifice.

Strained red knots tied around every passing tree,
the pull keeps my torso from the dirt
and yet this beast has already made it to the waters.

The low gurgle, the watering mouth,
my hand is sinking, my body
an expression of war,
and once my head rolls back to meet the throat,
the beast,

a snap from my chest–my eyes have gone red.
I swear the skies are screaming for us.

detachment felt of a sword
and a quick easy swallow into the depths of the lake.

There's blood in the water,
and I–

lost the rest.

Loathe

The skin beneath me is plastered in grease.
A pale excuse for a man.
I can trace down his figure with delicate fingers
and find myself filled with rage when met
with such rough skin–lubricated like slug
as if the insides were too gruesome to truly keep trapped.

Blonde hair and blue eyes never favored him,
so when graced with a compliment out of pity
he would relish in it for a century.
As if spouting such thin words could convince near ears to
forget their eyes.

I never understood the sharp blades of hate
until I saw the artificial crown
placed unpleasantly upon his head,
by his own hand.

Distasteful words, disgraceful actions.
He does not deserve the words, nor the rage.
Still, my screams deserve to be seen.

Hunger in threes

I am starving.
I roll onto my stomach, bunching up a pillow under me.
Odd, how this stinging pain can overtake my body and make me
still.
I can't move, my blood feels slower, and my head hurts,
and I don't know what it wants. I can't breath
I can't think, I am only hunger,
only sharp pains and needs.
A starved animal. Trying to get up.

My hands, I see, are golden.
They are dripping constantly–asking, waiting, imagining.
I hardly understand them, but I would give them my life.
These tips could weave out any dream,
through ink, paint, or plastic.
I can touch something and experience a world,
I can touch your hand; send a thought
and you'll get the idea, the feeling.

The thin layer of sweat on your palm haunts me;
the corner of your lip, the glance of your eye.
Thoughts of you overwhelm me until my muscles tire.
I want to create worlds in your name,
planetary bodies that spin and make history for themselves.
But I can't pick up a pen. I can't settle on the words.
I'll appreciate my own dips and curves the way I do yours,
I'll hold myself and hug myself until you are here again,
and that simple touch feels enough like writing words about
you
to satiate this for now.

Butterfly Loin

watch the ink spread

The Floor

Maybe gravity is hitting me harder these days.
Not enough blood to my brain to make it function right.
It's pooling in my feet, making me ache, reminding me of the
weight.
I think laying down would be better.

The hiss between my red cheek and the numbing concrete
repelling one another, as they tend to
make a harsher impact than previously discussed.
I can hear the blood rushing from my neck
to my skull, right behind the ears
that can't seem to descry anything else.

My heart is fighting for something.
The rapid rhythmic muscle desperate to lift me,
ascend me towards the heavens, talks of power
this motionless place of need, each intake of blood
halts the body, like a locked lung of air,
unable to move until its owner lets go.

The floor shines, as if wet, reflecting a sharp light
through my tired eyes, I track a slow particle of dust
as it keeps its distance while moving over my head,
and I allow my eyes to roll back until swallowed
somewhere deep in the mind, the place where I sense
the stillness of my limbs, their place on this earth.
Delicately, now, replaced with air.
The molecules in fingertips begin to disperse, until
I can no longer feel anything, until I am dust
swirling along the floor.

Becoming another layer to this concrete.

Nose blind II

Inhale
the moss and grass that saturate
this bare muggy air.
A faint moment of citrus,
oak, then amber,
and a spicy unexplainable thing.
Various greens, whipping by;
pine, sage, jade–
a foresty glorious feat.

Exhale
and run a little further. A little harder.
Deepen your breath for more,
until the lungs grow hot and sharp,
until the flame thaws your chest;
your heart;
the earth inside of you.

The unearthing of you.
Reach your arms out for fist fulls
of leaves, branches, flowers.
It may hurt, but look at them,
feel them, smell them.
Keep running until you fall,
and then run again.

A Poet

If I am a poet;
Let me curl up in a cool dry place.
For you, to take bits of me, slowly
crush me, between two stones made for each other.
Use me, to nourish, eat, drink, sprinkle on top.

If I am a poet;
Taste the words I have yet to give you.
Make breads from the powders of my blood and bones,
as variety meats, ripened by tenderness,
cure in salts, sliced thin and ready.

If I am a poet;
Tie my limbs up with twine.
Pick from me generously, daily.
As I will lay brittle, I will lay bare,
if it means to be here, with you.

Because, if I am a poet, I must be sweet,
there must be more to me than I can see.
And if you find me useful, if you find me a poet,
then maybe, I will finally know how you feel about me.

Red string III

My knees fall, crashing into the mud,
my hands try to protect my heart, my chest,
gripping at the fabric on my shoulders as if it will help.
For a moment, I look up,
allowing fresh waters to cleanse the salt from my face.
A ping, again, within the chest causes a cold rushed inhale,
And I–

can feel the burning sensation fill my throat, as
the air escapes by a force sharper than arrows.
The pressure builds in my head,
I can only see red–only feel cold.
The weight of the wet fabric begins to pull me to the earth.

I lay still in the mud, watching the land become drenched,
smelling the washing of all but my insides.
A dove lands in distant view,
as hear strings scratch deeper and deeper
begging my chest to open into its voided refuge.

The burning in my chest, in my hands, in my stomach,
is begging me to run.
As if it will cleanse me, or free me from this ache.
My skin caked in mud,
my chest dripping blood,
and the rain continues down to wash it all away.

I will reach that dove,
keep its heart in a safe place.

Lost Dog

You've run away again, from this repetitious dwelling,
leaving the door ajar, so I can see
the spectral autonomy of your white dress–
flowing a stream of light behind you, as
your shins lick the tall grass in your way and
your bare feet hook into each muddy step.

Your laughter sizzles through the evening mist
showing me that rare hallucination, again
as lengthy white dog, pushing your nose into the land
digging, endlessly, digging,
looking to fill some incomprehensible craving.

I've seen you unearth various hearts, hare and human,
wrapping them delicately in your jaw and carrying them home,
no puncture wound, even near your sharpest gold tooth.
You only tried to kindle safety; separating from the body, and
guarding beneath your own soil.

I watch you run into these evenings clean, and return
half soaked at dawn, brown and red staining your white,
only the trail of your hot breath allows me to find you this way.

Oh sweet dog, if this grass begins to lay too weary for your
soiled feet,
let me carry you to the window and show you
how it reflects the light you cast
over these hills, through each sigh
a whistle will sing to the birds that
have yet to understand their true meaning, as I

may never understand mine. But yours is far greater than any I could bear.

Thank you
to my dear friends and my dear lover

A Glimpse of the Author

"Natalya Ziska (he/she) is a multi-disciplinary artist living in Portland Oregon.

Having self-published under a pseudonym in the past, Ziska is finally stepping into the light under his name, unveiling a collection that erupts in a gorgeous violence— visceral, feral, and unflinchingly raw.

Drenched in desire, tangled in guttural anguish, and the captured texture of memories as ephemeral and soft, as whispers in the dark–Ziska speaks in a language that permeates the mind; words that grip you in their teeth, where you are bound to remain.

Her poetic instincts as carnal and rabid as the animalistic perspectives she embodies - effortlessly delivers readers to a place that is deeply, unmistakably human. This exhilarating collection carves a deeply delicate balance, juxtaposing the intensities of love and rage with unmatchable grace."

-Charlie Faulkner